Before She Was Harriet

LESA CLINE-RANSOME

illustrated by

JAMES E. RANSOME

Holiday House 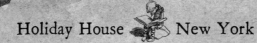 New York

Here she sits
an old woman
tired and worn
her legs stiff
her back achy

but before wrinkles formed
and her eyes failed
before she reached
her twilight years
she could walk for miles
and see clearly
under a sky lit only with stars

Before she was an old woman
she was a *suffragist*
a voice for women
who had none
in marriages
in courts
in voting booths
before her voice became
soft and raspy
it was loud
and angry
rising above injustice

Na

Before she was a *suffragist*
she was *General Tubman*
rising out of the fog
armed with courage
strong in the face of rebels
and planters and overseers
as they watched
fields burn
and bridges fall
and 700 slaves
stop chopping
and start running
to a woman
who ferried them
to freedom
on the Combahee River
turned River Jordan

Before she was
General Tubman
she was a *Union spy*
carrying secrets
across battlefields
to soldiers
fighting in the Civil War
for President Lincoln
to end slavery

Before she was a
Union spy
she was a *nurse*
caring for those hit
with bullets
and hatred
and fear
tending to them
with bandages
and words
in the bloodied dirt of
southern soil

Before she was a *nurse*
she was *Aunt Harriet*
daughter of Ben and Rit
who helped her parents
flee their master
and find their way
through woods and streams
to the safety of Canada
and a new home
in the north

Before she was *Aunt Harriet*
she was *Moses*
a conductor
on an Underground Railroad
with no trains
and no tracks
just passengers
traveling to freedom
up north
through swamps
past slave catchers
across rivers
under the cover of night

seeking the promised land
for her people
led by dreams
and God
and faith
a wisp of a woman
with the courage
of a lion

Before she was *Moses*
she was *Minty*
of Maryland
of one slave owner
and then others
who worked her
punished her
with lashes
broke her back
but not her spirit

Before she was *Minty*
she was *Araminta*
a young girl
taught by her father
to read
the woods
and
the stars
at night
readying
for the day

she'd leave behind
slavery
along with her name
and pick a new one
Harriet

and remember
her days
as a *suffragist*
as a *General*
as a *spy*
as a *nurse*
as *Aunt Harriet*
as *Moses*
as a *conductor*

as *Minty*
as *Araminta*
who dreamed
of living long enough
to one day
be old
stiff and achy
tired and worn and wrinkled
and *free*

To the guiding force of all the women who have led the way through courage, strength, perseverance, and intellect—Harriet Tubman, Sojourner Truth, Fannie Lou Hamer, Toni Morrison, Michelle Obama, Viola Davis, Anne Sneed, Ernestine Cline.—L. C.-R.

To black women who have carried the weight of family and work with grace and dignity.—J. R.

HOLIDAY HOUSE is registered in the U.S. Patent and Trademark Office
Printed and bound in March 2017 at Toppan Leefung, DongGuan City, China.
www.holidayhouse.com
First Edition
1 3 5 7 9 10 8 6 4 2

Library of Congress Cataloging-in-Publication Data
Names: Cline-Ransome, Lesa, author. || Ransome, James, illustrator.
Title: Before she was Harriet : the story of Harriet Tubman / by Lesa
Cline-Ransome ; illustrated by James Ransome.
Description: First edition. || New York : Holiday House, [2017] || Audience:
004–008.
Identifiers: LCCN 2016051680 || ISBN 9780823420476 (hardcover)
Subjects: LCSH: Tubman, Harriet, 1820?–1913—Juvenile literature. ||
Slaves—United States—Biography—Juvenile literature. || African
Americans—Biography—Juvenile literature. || African American
women—Biography—Juvenile literature. || Underground Railroad—Juvenile
literature.
Classification: LCC E444.T82 C56 2018 || DDC 973.7115092 [B] —dc23 LC record available at https://lccn.loc.gov/2016051680